OVER THE ANVIL WE STRETCH

BY ANIS MOJGANI

Over the Anvil We Stretch

Anis Mojgani

Write Bloody Publishing ©2008

1st printing.

Printed in NASHVILLE TN USA

Cover Designed by Cole Nuckols

Illustrations by Anis Mojgani

Interior Layout by Lea C. Deschenes

Edited by Saadia Byram, Derrick Brown and Michael Edward Sarnowski

WRITEBLOODY
QUALITY AMERICAN BOOKS AND PRINTING

Over the Anvil We Stretch

ONE

Dedication

for the magnolias of new orleans,

the honeysuckle on my grandparents' walls,

and for sarah who helped find me

on days when I wanted to stay lost

When the rain hits the snake in the head,

he closes his eyes and wishes he were

asleep in a tire on the side of the road,

so young boys could roll him over, forever.

— Frank Stanford

A pitchfork fell from the sky. It fell like a struck crow. It hit the earth and broke into large dust. A small boy took the broken pieces, their atoms murmuring, and in the dark swallowed them. The slivers dropped like lightning into his gut, scratching his throat on the way down. The boy sat on his knees before he went to bed. Trying to sleep, he tossed like a thundercloud. His organs grinding the piecemeal pitchfork into the pieces of himself, the bits of it moving through him, eeking out the sound of metal across bone and skin. The sky came in closer to listen to the song his body was making. He curled like an armadillo, arms wrapped around himself tight as a tomb, trying to both claw the song out of his belly and to protect it. Across the sky's shoulders he scraped his palms until he was too tired to bleed from them, his body so soft that everything hurt. On the other side of his life, the river moved like a dark instrument. A long cello wailing softly and longly, waiting for him to move his fingers through it.

ONE
We were horses

The black clouds and the stars
that danced between them, were a carnival.
And we were the kids born of it.

when I was sick

I bit down. Broke the thermometer in my mouth.

The mercury coated my stomach in silver. I swallowed a bird.

He pecked his songs across the metal of my silver belly.

The notes echoed through my throat and outside. He made

the beautiful things that flew out from me. But the melodies

twisted too much. They kept me up at night. So I climbed outside

and sat in a field. I watched the spiders, fat on rain water, crawl

over the wet grass, and filled a jar with them. Swallowed the jarful.

The bird swallowed them as well. Grew fat. Too fat to move.

Could only peck out one note. The same note. Incessant.

I couldn't sleep. I heard the bird's song like the ghost of a telegraph

rolling over and over inside of me, over and over and out of me.

He filled my walls with the chatter. So I swallowed a cat to eat the bird.

He did, and then curled up to sleep. Now I had a cat dreaming in my gut.

He rubbed his paws over my bones, sharpening them, thinking of

too many trees to climb, painting the hunt the taste the soft chitter

of the mouse. I began understanding the fabric of the sky, the gulp

of the night. The cat told me *God is concave. Blake was a burning*

feather filled with the angelic light. What are you, a backyard deity?

A small oven hell. He quoted to me the Russians--snuck the liquor in,

got drunk till dawn. I've never read the Russians. That cat made my head hurt.

I coughed up his wet fur. I thought *I think I'm getting sick.* He didn't care.

He began painting the bodies of persimmons, spoke with an accent.

He called for peacocks and pomegranates. *Peacocks! Pomegranates!*

This cat's visions were making me nauseous. I started eating strawberries.

Gorged myself on them. I was trying to shove my whole body out.

I filled the inside of me with the fruit, felt my organs being pushed out.

Throwing myself up through my fingernails, thrown through the knees

the neck, my teeth turning red. Nothing but strawberries. I felt the cat leave.

The heart leave. Both lungs, everything ever placed between the ribs

and under my skin. All pushed out. Nothing but the strawberries.

They ate me from the inside out. Left nothing. All of me became seeds,

my body sung in seeds. I filled the soft black earth with the song.

The parts of me my parents put together were put back into the world.

The birds perching on the fence posts came and picked me up.

They held me in their beaks and fed me to their young, the eyes

still shut with skin, too blind to see what they were eating.

4 stars

there was a wasp nest on the back porch

it looked like dead honeycomb

outside

was a hornet's hive

I stuck my hand in there

the sun buzzed loudly

nothing could bite me

a caterpillar did

I climbed its tree

it kissed me with its back

its hair was sharp enough to leave four stars in my palm

the world spun through my hands

it had crashed into our street

so I picked it up

in the shed at the back of the backyard

I found a giant

he was sleeping

while he hummed I told him my dreams

then led him back into our yellow kitchen

I loved the smell of the air conditioner

there was one in the dining room

and one in my parents' bedroom

putting my face in front of the vents

made me feel like sunday

I could bike the whole square of the block in two minutes flat

Jalal

Put and Rue lived around the corner from us

there was a tree in front of their house

it was too big to be a birch

Samandar was only one fence hop away

his mother showed mine what God looked like

God smelled like my father

both their beards were black bears

me and mom went fishing in the park

I caught two catfish

and waited for them to die

they swam in circles inside the refrigerator

because I had never learned how to kill anything

in Mississippi

we ate all three perch I had caught

the grasshoppers there?

they are big as an almond joy

my sister

had a pet rat

part of his ear was gone

his name was Pierre

I named my mouse after a favorite book

Charlotte's Web

she is buried under a white rock

the day our dog died

pops found him hanging from the clothesline

I cried into my pillow

I was ten years old

I could fit under the house

my knees didn't care

neither did the dark

after the tub

the hallway from the bath's room to mine

was a black tunnel

breathing only to swallow me

I shivered and was more afraid of that walk

than anything ever since

even now

there are moments where it still shakes me

but there were times where the night

sat beside me on my bed

quietly

like it was a big man

who had to do what I told him to

he was too dumb

or he loved me too much

either way he had the same smile

I ain't never been stung by a bee before

not my whole life

from my window

the toads were heard every night

in the summer behind the house

mating by the thousands

the night sky loved this

would watch it happening

and winked slowly through the long months

we were horses

I was in a dream country. You were there.

And all those little blonde hairs that run up your legs

and over your shoulders.

the manual

squeeze 20 grapes in your cheeks

bite down

spit watermelon seeds

I bet you five pieces you can't spit em further than me

kick a can

chase trains

wave at strangers

drive an imaginary submarine

make one out of a box

sleep on a floor with a blanket and a lantern

draw birds

live forever

plant a tree

write your fist on a wall

run for no reason down the middle of the block

laugh at something funny

smile at sweetness

hold your fingers around it so it doesn't fall

find a dark row in a movie theater

and make out with me

your kisses are a game of horseshoes

I wish I were playing

beneath the stars fat and wet with light

high in the full black sky

so big and silent

it can carry us through this crazy thing

dance under it

listen for the sounds the fields make

the tongues the trees are speaking in

the love the leaves are making with the wind

swallow it down

this is church

your teeth tiny doors

s.j.h.

The herd of salamanders started off with the mandolin. It was black
and curled in on itself when the strings popped. She needed a voice
so the stars whispered and offered up their shoulders to the fire.
The salamanders had a bowl of pears. One of them said *These are
delicious, let us make a heart of them.* They peeled the pears, sliced
them up and with the mandolin and the stars' shoulders gently placed
the pieces into the flames. One of the salamanders was wearing a necklace.
It had a simple silver chain with a panda on the end, in it went. *It will keep
her close to the bears in her spine, the ones that will hold her for all the years
that she won't know her father, and once he comes and goes again, in her sleep
the bears will still hold her close.*

The moon shines down on the salamanders. They do not know so much
what they are doing but none of the animals on this planet do. We pick up
pieces of ourselves, put them in the fire, and see what comes out. They gather
threads together and throw in dinner plates round as sundials, so this girl
they are making can hold time like it was food--swallow down every drop
of it and keep it trapped inside against her lungs. They make her lungs
out of the silver tails of foxes and the laughter of old men. She will take
big breaths like wishes and keep them close, before pushing them
into the air. Her feet, they make from a secret, passed between ears.

Her hands, the softest clay they can find. Her eyes are small rivers.

They pour them in with painted teapots then put the teapots in as well.

The moon breathes in, looks down on the salamanders dancing wild

round their kitchen, and then comes down to join her. The moon gives

her its sunlight, to make sure her legs are always warm.

undertaker

you hold my body like a ghost

left foot in the grave

right fingers in heaven

unfortunately

I'll love one until

she loves me so hard that I

want to be alone

in the funeral parlor

he clears the wood

big trunks of it

they look like grey stone

he wipes his brow

swings an axe

and pulls the branches

dragging them across the fields

he is supposed to burn them

one of these days he will

for now he pauses

he eats a sandwich

stands one leg on a dead tree

with one arm on the leg

stares into the sky

it is late afternoon

and he can see a ghostly dollar of a moon

already starting to make itself known

to the quiet silver of the sun

he finishes his lunch

and continues

stripping the woods of this world

the seasons

your back

comes up

like a new field

full of something that ain't been grown before

something the night

can't wait to harvest

it wants to open you up right now

it knows by the time

the season for you comes

nothing'll be left but the fruit to pull

stay in the barn

in the summertime

the shadows sleep in the beams with the swallows

we collected their feathers from the straw

filled our pillows with them

stuffed our beds with their bodies

keeping them close to us

to keep the barn door closed

it takes heavy timber set against the door

the women and men

they struggle

to hear one another inside themselves

the horses

he bought her a pair of white gloves

they are somewhere in a car or a box

his lawn is drowning in leaves

he thinks he can feel something in his gut

it is a little ache of a little man

washing his hands under soft water

the little man has been here before

he sighs so his chest don't cave inward

his throat catches

a house somewhere is disappearing

the knight of swords is upside down

the boy stays up past his bedtime

listening to the emptiness move its shoes across the floor

it sounds like nothing

the boy doesn't like this

he puts music on

it only makes him feel worse

shadows of worms moving inside

the ghosts of horses

the girl is already preparing her birds for flight

the boy feels the something of this in his gut

he has been here before

the birds are soft

she is clipping their nails

clipping their feathers

she misses him

and wraps a blanket around her breast

to keep it warm when all of it all happens

she is putting her gloves on

the grass outside is drowning in gold

the gold breaks under shuffling feet

the ghosts neigh silent

the boy wishes the world moved differently

the girl's song is precious to him

his fingers miss their notes

the stars

they do not care

they have horses of their own to tether

inside the boy

the little man

done washing

dries his little hands

prays a little prayer

he has been here before

he has holes in his skin

the wind will be on its way soon enough to start blowing through another one

fireworks

before I go

I'll burn in the backyard
all the bags of leaves my bedroom has collected

I'll ride my bike all week long
and somewhere between the hands and the stones

bury the kneecaps of God
I don't want to see any memories

I spend my days making paper airplanes by myself
my heart tracing ghosts
on the inside of my skull

everything I own reminds me of something else
I need a new skin
this one's still uncomfortable

I wish I could play the banjo and talk to snakes

libraries make me safe and sad at the same time

they feel like the breaths of people I've known

if you talk to her tell her

I been learning new things

without fear of the teeth

I pet a dog I didn't know

his coat o how it does shine

he doesn't always know where to go

or what to do

there are fishhooks in his skin

and an accordion from somewhere

that he swears could be the moonlight in a white mustache

sometimes he feels like a phony

that he laughs out of clumsiness

that his skeleton doesn't like the sound his heart makes at night

and wishes

to run away

out over the ridges

falling into place amongst the silhouetted woods

the trees all know to grow in the same direction

the rivers

they know these same things

he wants to write something soft and meaningful

he wants to make birds that like the feel of their feathers in the wind

for those wings to mean everything

and to give them to you

the trees all know which direction to grow

the axe sits in the stump

waits for a hand

the spoons sit in their drawer

waiting for soup

the rain is warm in heaven

I lay in the dust and made wings out of my arms.

The farmer bled behind the barn.

He had shot 3 arrows into his chest.

His wife cried over his heart,

peeled it out of his skin, fed it to the birds.

They found my mother. She slept.

They rubbed their wings into her eyes.

My father saw those green feathers

and felt music burning his throat.

He leaked himself into her ear.

Songs stirred inside.

A blue horse was bucking inside the fence of an ugly countryside.

I found a field to bury myself back inside of.

Our rivers snaked through it.

My river is the Mississippi.

Mercury was the cigarette of a god.

I was a coyote.

The streets are still deserts.

The sun buzzes loudly.

I pulled up an entire field of grass,

placing those green blades to my mouth,

trying to turn them into a cricket harp.

All I made was spit.

My childhood was so beautiful that sometimes

I break things.

My red house burned bright.

I took its ashes, made a red cap from them.

The man in the white suit

watches movies in the dark when a child dies.

He weeps out loud and has put on his dark tie.

Tomorrow he will return to his garden and his farm.

I was the beard of a billy goat.

God was in the billy goat.

God was in the cornbread.

The cornbread was in the pig.

The poets don't eat the pig.

The pig eats the apple.

Peel one.

Find a boy to give the skin to.

Save your bread.

Give it to the ducks.

I found the farmer in a black face between the books of Saint Mark.

He was still bleeding.

I licked his fingers. They tasted like mine.

My head was hot

my hair wet.

I took off my red hat and gave it to you.

You swallowed it.

Said, this will keep me warm.

It turned your hair black.

My red house is still burning.

You have shoulders that tell me this.

I lay in the dust and waved my arms,

made dirt angels for you.

I'm trying to leave this earth behind

but my pockets are filled with it.

swallowing hatchets, handle first

there is someplace where he doesn't recognize anybody's voice, and it's here

where he wishes he were right now.

TWO

Behind the farm

Wandering under the floorboards of our childhood,
I found a whistle and blew it.
Only the animals could hear it.

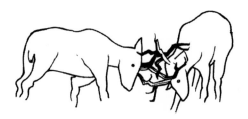

Antarctica

it was me and seven puppies

Gus named them after the continents

I was to take the smallest

and hold it in a sack underwater

I didn't want to know what that felt like

so I carried her through the woods

and left her out there

told everyone

she struggled at first

but then she went limp like half a bag of flour

and was still.

and then I buried her.

sack and all.

on the way back in

I went over the words in my head

made sure it all sounded right

I dug up a patch of earth

and put the empty sack in there

even found a white rock

to push down on top to mark it

like it was a real grave and all

that night after everyone went to bed

from out between the dark trees

north of the house

I could hear the whimper of the dog

I put the pillow over my head

her cry was slight

and almost too high to catch

but it still pawed against my ears

and kept pawing until I fell asleep

and couldn't hear her anymore

inside the limo

before Pee-Wee's funeral

we drove by his parents' house

to help them drive stuff over

when his father opened the door to the back seat

in his black hands there was a tray of donuts

covered in cellophane

the man was wearing a suit

and even though I had never seen him before

something about him

made it seem like this wasn't his usual wear

I remember him looking cheap in it

or perhaps at that age I could just tell the cheapness

of a cheap suit itself

he told us to help ourselves to the donuts and things

I wanted one badly

but didn't take one

something in my mother's face told me I shouldn't

that it was inappropriate

or perhaps at that age I could just tell

that when people are filled with sorrow

even if it was just a donut

I didn't want to feel like

I was taking something else from them

the moccasins

there are moccasins in the river

the water moves against their sides

as they slide through the current

there are wolves everywhere

you told me God was a patch of galaxy

moving inside the trapped bodies of a boy and girl

riding on the back of a wolf through space

you pulled ink out of me

when all I thought left were stems

from flowers I had given away

you fought for this

for these words

you bit your tongue

put it in my mouth

and bled into me

your blood

beats red and fast

strong and weak kneed

hoping

waiting

for someone

to swim inside of it

letting it dry over their shoulders and say:

this what you are is mine

it is now what me is

my rivers are not broken

they are long

there are bones buried in the bottom of their black mud

and flowers floating above them

somewhere in the middle

you swim

on your back

arms spread out

waiting for the stars to pull you back into them

and for me to take your hand

come

take mine

I said before

there are wolves everywhere

let us catch one

and take it back to its home

she is still gone

and the only music playing

is nothing and the dogs sleeping

sharpen the lances

I know that there may be wars inside your head on some days

and how

some of them

you're gonna have to fight alone

but I pray that if the darkness comes big and too big and sharp

I'll see you down there

brother of mine

there are swamps that we come from

children of the cypress knee

sister

it's okay to run

I learned that long ago

I ain't been still since

it don't mean I don't love you

I'm just trying to catch up to my heart

I've let it out of my hands too many times

I have to learn how to hold it tighter

there are hungry birds that fly around us all

THREE
Song of the axe

When we dug the days out of the dirt I held you with both my hands.

the gardenias

The Gardener and I are sitting in the pews of the train station.

He one over and on its far end--with one glove on and one glove

on the pew, a clutch of gardenias sitting in the flat of its palm.

We sit here and I stare straight ahead, stare through the walls

and stare at the ceilings, searching for ceiling fans.

Searching for spirits in the ceiling. I stare down, and the Gardener

stares me down. The pupils of my eyes move to their corners,

like the nose of mice peeking past, and catch the light in the peripheral.

I try to count the tiles on the floor but the tiles, they are only colored bits

of color and sediment. Broken, pushed, and pressed together.

There is a big clock on the wall. It doesn't move.

The dust particles itself in the air between the atoms,

and the glow in this place carries itself in a lonely way. We sit here

waiting for the trains, the roots of the gardenias clinging with dirt,

and the Gardener....

He wears a cap on that glowing head.

The cap it is a dark one.

her kiss a shovel

1

she dresses herself in a mystery

curses soap

when she bathes

she lets the water pour over her body alone

and only washes her hair

2

there are many bodies

that tremble between his trees

he wants to bury them

inside that graveyard she pulls

over her shoulders

he wants to push his fingers through her skin

swallow her whole

3

the dogs outside walk through the streets

there are no collars round their necks

they are sniffing for bones they want bones

full moon tonight

he feels like a shadow and the trees they don't talk out loud anymore

the axe man

there is a man walking beneath the air

he is carrying an axe

dragging the blade through the fields

to find the blood

the fields are empty

so is the sky

only grey getting darker

the wrists get heavy on backwards nights

when the day is longer

and keeps looking around instead of ahead

I can't find a riverbank to save my life he thinks

there is nothing buried here

there is nothing to bury

and no place to bury it

all the animals find another way to get into heaven

the jackrabbits

are scrawling their names on the pink walls of the bathroom

the raccoons on the back fence

they are all using parts of me I thought were long dead

You gave them up

I didn't know

where are they? give them back to me

they are mine

You found a beautiful space far from you to put them inside of

where is that space

We sniffed them out

Promised to hold them

to show them again what touch can mean

Come outside

Let the clouds do the same to you

the man keeps dragging the axe behind him

he is crying

where am I

there is a syrupy blackness coming in on the nightfall

he can taste it in the wind and hesitant rain

he thinks that maybe tonight he will dig up the weeds out back

break the branches off of the trees that scrape his window

and make them into arrows

shoot the clouds down

bleed them dry

take the cotton of their carcasses

plant it

and grow an orchard from their bodies

WHERE AM I?

he screams

he screams and screams

and drags his axe over and over the ground beneath him

pulling up soil

bits of shell

but no water

and no bones

these foxes

there is nothing here for me

but still I scrabble at the blade

gamble the wheat

let loose the dogs

just to see if they can find my scent

amongst the willows

I pour kerosene over the roots

wade through the water

and double back around

but we

the dogs and I

we both know which way Orion is facing

we both know which way I will take

we have been down this trail before

we have poured this milk

licked this bowl

felt the taste of porcelain on our tongue

broken a bit of brimstone

and rubbed the corn

into our paws

when the cotton bales are set on fire

we have drawn closer to the heat

I have burnt tomorrow

but have filled my pockets with its ashes

like it was yesterday

felt the weight on my legs

carried them

like they were something

that had already passed

the iron rooster doesn't turn

the night is still

there is no point in throwing anything into it

empty

there ain't nothing here but the wind

the black

and the something of something holy

gone

hoping to come back

from out the sky

the fat man's face

is drinking from my body tonight

taking more than his share

more than what

he's supposed

to take

he drinks heavily

licks the side of the bowl

he makes sounds

like an animal trying to break

out of its wooden skin

the devil's on a stump

but he ain't no friend of mine

but neither is his father neether

the bitten cartographer
believes in hair of the dog

under the clouds my arms are mumbling

I don't pay them much mind

I think a lot about love

and what body it's gonna come in

don't fuck me

I'm not that good of a conversationalist

I hear too many things

that other people can't see

I wish I didn't

but this equilibrium thing

is a waterlogged scorpion

I stare at ceilings

searching for maps that lead outside

if you talk to me with your body

and I ain't listening

it's cuz my nose is sniffing

for the window that opens

if you want me

I won't be there

my ankles'll be searching for the nearest river

must be the animal inside

it comes out with the lust

walks around

in this here skin of mine

bites your tongue

licks the sweat

rubs the blood

that moves inside your back

my senses heighten

I can smell the sky

spinning outside

between your bed

and the distance to the heavens

you'll hear the howl of my heart

I'll hear the clouds

laughing back at my prayers

poem

I want to kiss your breast

so much more

than writing any of these here poems

the owls

nothing comes

not the ghosts

not the sorrow

only a vapid emptiness

a long quiet of a man

sipping from a cup

and shifting the pages at his desk

some fall into his lap

he leaves them there

when he stands

they fall to the floor

like fish from the news

he doesn't even pull out a knife

to clean them of their bones

he doesn't even hear

when the mice do it for him

swallowing the eyes

taking the silver skins

to wear over their shoulders like the moon

hiding their thin hands

from the owls outside

the man stares out the window

watches the black confusion of the birds

and sees a thousand little scrapes of light

running over the earth

the kitchen knives

Suge buried all of his in the backyard

buried em blade up

they looked like little white shoots

just starting to appear

he said

he's goin catch himself something with this new crop

he don't know what

be it an angel

or something dressed up in the skin of a raccoon

but dammit something with blood inside of it

the spirits lay their traps, I'll lay mine

my father's machete was rusted all over

both sides of the blade

I took it from the back porch

knotted a bit of string around its black handle

and tied it to the clothesline in the backyard

I strung another string to the line

ran it inside and through the loop of a metal bell

I hung the bell over the foot of my bed

round a quarter past one

the bell twitched

I went out the backdoor

the moon's cold light was all over the garden

it made the cucumbers on the ground look like little white statues

I held my breath when I walked past them

I heard it struggling

it was on the end of the blade

I grabbed it by the back of its head

fist full of fur

I had to mind its teeth

it squealed and it squirmed

spat in the air

clawing at my wrists

looking nothing like what the stories said

it got some good scratches in

I pulled hard

it twisted in my hand like a knifed pig

it was gonna break its own neck

I took the machete in my other hand

and finished it

its cry got snagged in its throat

made a sound like a child's toe coming off

I wiped the blade on the grass

and tied the handle back on the line

I wiped my hands on my leg

and walked towards the house

I stumbled through the white cucumbers

and heard it make a soft whimper

I'll skin it in the morning

I sighed and opened the screen door

got the gauze out from under the sink

rocking back and forth I washed the blood from my arms

and the grey hairs

that had stuck to my fingers

behind the lodge

gather the deer heads

strip the horns from their skulls

the man out back is bloody

and carries his hammer loosely

it is wet

do me next

after I punched him in the mouth
the man in the dream said:

HE BROKE 3 OF MAH TEETH

AH WAS ON MAH KNEES

THE SUN WAS CUTTIN THE SIDEWALK

HIS FIST TURNED MAH TEETH INTO SUGAR

THAHS WHEN HE RAN

DOWN THE STREET

BETWEEN THE BUILDINS

AHM BEHINDIM

RUNNIN HARD

WE LL FINDIM BACK OF THE TREES

BREAK HIS SHOULDERS

AND DRINKIM DOWN

MAH RAZORS IN MY BOOT

ITS BEEN LOOKIN FUR A NAME

WHATEVER HIS IS

AHLL GIVIT TO THE RAZOR

THIS AINT

EVEN

HIS TOWN

in the middle of the day the south was black and bright

they were chasing me

I needed to get away and I left them behind
running

but it took more muscle than I had to move my leg
and everything in my body was slow as I saw two more come running around
      the corner down the block
fast and faster than I was
and where were you?

I lost you somewhere
I needed to save you

we were in the south
grass dead green and yellow growing wide between houses
porches of wooden slats flat to the ground
the sun in large strips between buildings
and there was a bar in the daylight
that all of us had come out of

into a street that this country had forgotten

if it ever knew that it was here

we were laughing like it was against the law

this town didn't want none of that

and that's where he was

I swear he wanted to kill me

I hit him

he split like a necklace

and that's when I took off

I heard nothing but the song in my ears

moving like a deaf man's lips

bright light chanty

most nights all I'd like to do is climb a tree somewhere

swallow the top branches

to try to scratch this song

that is stuck somewhere between

the skin and the heart

the angel is clapping loudly above

I want to move inside of someone

it is cold out here

I wake from dreaming

and can still smell the smell of bodies burning

FOUR

Under the wolf,
the fawns slept

Throwing the tubwater out every evening,
the water was still warm when it touched the flowers.

the Barrels

One day, people will look back at this moment in history and say, 'Thank God there were coura-geous people willing to serve, because they laid the foundations for peace for generations to come.

—GW

when the barrels were full of rainwater
we would put them on the wagon
the horses bridled up and ready to go

as our seats would jostle in the bumps of the road
we would smoke cigarettes
and make jokes about the girls we longed to fuck

along the way
men in their yards
would stop and smile
nod their heads at us in approval
little boys would stare
some of them would salute
we saluted back with a laugh and a wink
the women would come out of their doors

swoon

and wave their white handkerchiefs

we passed the dark bottle between us

we would finally make our way to the cemetery
and slowly through its gates

as we rolled under the black arch
we buttoned the top two buttons of the uniform
and stared down the hill
the bodies all marked
with the same white posts

the posts sticking straight up out of the grass
they looked like markers
so the planes would know where to land
except there was no space for that

we made our way down the paths
at every row we'd stop
to empty the barrels out
over each one of the graves
give the boys a drink

as we poured the water

we would laugh about those ladies with the kerchiefs

and what we would do with them later tonight in town

what the sweat on their thighs tasted like

by the time we finished with the barrels

dusk would be settling in

as we made our way out

in the distance

over the top of the far side of the valley

we could see the silhouette of the towers

red lights blinking

keeping track of the new bodies coming in

in the echo of the darkness

fresh and wet

the coffin makers would be starting their shift

the ring of the hammer on the nail rising over the trees

the sound

of the cheap slats of pine being boxed together

we couldn't hear it of course

the wagon's wheels always creaked

we just knew the sounds were there

the whole town did

it's why every night we all got drunk and we all got fucked

and in the morning we would all sing the same song

look out the window

and pray the mist outside was just a fog

and not the ghosts we had made together

trying to come back to us

after the birds

1

I move to the country

take to wearing big boots

with shorts and a hat with a wide brim

grow out my beard again

come into town

on the wings of the town's tall tales of my spine of gold

and in the old dust of my red beat up truck

there are lightning bolts in my eyes

the elbow of the Devil curling in my smile

I pay for my food and supplies

always

with a bag of quarters

a sack of silver

I hold the front fanged tooth of a black coyote in my pocket

I tell the children it is an angel's

I won it in a bet

some days I tell them I won it in a fight

the scars on my hands as well

I stare out the window when I drive

radio off

looking at the sky

smiling at the way God made this world of His

we are little birds

2

the sun is mine

it is an orange

I grew it

I grow it every morning

slice it into quarters

drink its blood

I fill up on it

I sit up late

surrounded by the songs of toads

they make love in the pond

my house is wood

I am always working on it

hammering a windowsill

placing a ladder against it

I am surrounded by paint buckets

my house was once painted white

but now it is a whale of a home

skin peeling

brown bones peeking through in the day light

and whispering in the wind of the night

3

I'd dream of drinking the night away

collapse drunk in the fields

wake with seeds in my mouth

crows on my back

but I don't drink and some things

will not change

so instead

I stay in the barn all night long

sawing wood

the blade

back

and forth

like moving the arms of a boat

I am going somewhere

peeling a song out of the song of metal in wood

sharp on pulp

branch in mother

cutting time

into dust and sweat

piling it on the floor around me

chips

and slivers

planks and pieces

saw all night long

make piles of it all

they stack themselves where they fall

in the pocket of dark surrounding me

I saw until it falls away and my bloody sun returns

leaving me with enough of something

to build something

to climb my way out of here

Milos

let us take a sack of spray paint and spray paint over the paintings

let us dance through Paris

climb over the bricks

break the windows of the Louvre

kiss in its shadows

scrawl manifestos over the canvasses

write morse code over the sculptures

roll out a sleeping bag on its floor to sleep inside of

tell one another a story by flashlight

bury each other in the other

unearth everything from before

feed grapes to the ants

light fireworks in the fist of sleeping kings

kill a monarch

break back outside

spit in the Seine

find a wall to do all these same things to upon and up against

break its bricks

climb over them

and when the sirens scream

laugh loud hold my hand and run fast

run through these streets with me with a bunch of bottles a bucket of gasoline a bucket of rags and a mouthful of matches a pocketful of paintings a city of walls and a fresh faced batch of policemen to chase the fires we are lighting with a laugh and a shoulder of gold and a thought that the museums are cemeteries that the dead pay the walls to hold what they have so we can walk through what we once were while the children take their skulls and turn them into gardens to pluck for far fathers and farther stars that on some nights resemble an armless mother praying for her arms and on other nights look like cold rocks staring over us and every tooth we tear from our jaws to throw at the black gloved riot soldiers is another shadow we are trying to lose where every giggle is filled with lust let us laugh the night away and I will fuck you like you were a prayer that could save me by having my mouth wrapped around you and I will hold you afterwards like you were the pulpit and I was the sky and this love that danced between that hardness was that holy electric telephone line of holiness that those two things spoke through take me into your heart like I was a saint and you were a face of forgiveness blooming in a valley destined to sink further be a river with me be the storm be the front porch the dirt the dust in the road the bend in the path the heat in the south the heat in the boot be a bootfull of banjo strings a fistful of written songs a mouthful of chocolate dust when they come to take us stab them between the eyes do not take your hand from around mine make a fist with the other and punch spines like guilt spit swear kiss them like a grandmother howl open mouthed terror love filled and when they come to cut our hair and ask to hear penance come from inside of us say with me loud and trembling but loud and clear:

I have already emptied myself I am a pitcher waiting to be filled with night a bowl for plums

the plums have come I have emptied myself

I kissed regret goodbye took the hand of another backwards angel and rode backwards into the rain watching our footsteps galloping away behind us say this with me when the hangman of morrow comes to hang the sun in its daily execution

sarah.

we are apples,

our love is an arrow.

I am unbuttoning my shirt painting a circle over my heart

you

shoot straight

FIVE

When Prometheus came

The stars broke their bones when they fell to the earth.
We held them in our arms until morning came
and they had stopped shaking.

after they fell and after we found them

we cut them open like melons

ate em with our hands

juice running down our chins

wiped our fingers on our legs

when we was called for dinner

we all came in to set the table

and faces still sticky

kissed mama on her cheek

baptize

your body is a church

whose doors closed to me

I'm waiting

on your steps

trying not to tremble

I don't know any other place

to go and pray inside of

it's why

still

when I'm close to you

sometimes

my skeleton shivers electric

and sometimes

I shudder heavy in this heavy coat called mine

when I was a boy

I heard the song of a God

on my bedroom floor

singing out from between

my hands

clasped tight as a lock

your memory carries a similar tune

for the ghost of your heart

is a holy place

and as most holy places are

when you hold me inside of it

I feel like a child

walking in a field

with a sky singing like a holocaust of icebergs

we are plates of sorrow

polishing ourselves off

sometimes asking for more

I have my mouth sitting open

with nothing but this shaking shaking inside

from being so close to your feathers

that I know why the wind goes

and comes back

and I know how awkward the weathervane feels

in its iron throat

that all it can do to announce

the footsteps of kings

is to spin and spin

and spin

in the blue of your eyes

I feel small

I feel big enough to touch a myth

your skin baptized me

and no matter the turn or direction

every path I take is me trying

to find my way back to that river

I don't know any other place

to go and pray inside of

it's too quiet in the south tonight
tonight the grass makes the rules

there is a brown cricket on the bookshelf

he's not saying a word

the horses sleep

there's a barn that needs burning

the creek sleeps

the sky is still as a bone in the black dust

the toads sleep

the crows are licking their wings

I have been moving through myself

like a body through a sleeve

a nightgown in a window

and I pray mouthless words of thread

but I swear my heart is fabric

and o it shakes in its smoothness

the dog sleeps

while the world makes rules for the world to follow

like it was a frying pan under a hill

the sickle makes its own rules

watch

how it glints in the moonlight

how it shines like a one worded whisper

San Luis Obispo

Pretty blonde girl on the train, where are you going?

I'll get off there with you, if you would take me.

I am a good man, and I'll be good for you. If you

take me and hide me from this world, I'll never

come up from under your soft hands.

Let us take a small square of California,

of Greece, call it ours. I'll make a flag

from a pair of pants of mine, Plant fruit trees.

Say the hell to the sky the ocean the building

the train and the president. Tall pretty blonde girl

with the pretty face the pretty smile, I have bowls

filled with dreams, bowls big enough for two.

We don't need anything else. Turn your back

on the moon with me. If you let me kiss your arms

forever, I will fold the shirts and bring you tea.

You'll stitch the sleeves and I will sing songs to you.

While I scramble the eggs, turn your back on the moon

and wear tanktops with stripes, socks off. We will get a goat

--get a car!--and outrun the sunlight. They'll never catch us.

Pretty blonde girl with the pretty eyes, the pretty eyes, the roads

were made for you and I. Let us follow one over the sea to where the olives grow in groves. Where the rocks are white and the grass

hard. I could build you a house if you let me learn how to, if you'll

help me hold the nails between my teeth. I am searching for dirt

to stand inside of. A mountain to whistle on. The field that will scream

gold so loud, the heart will stop talking so much. Take this one of mine.

Touch it. Poke its soft walls. It may jump back at first. But it wants your

hands to come to it in the night. It is something that was made for that.

So pretty blonde girl with the pretty teeth and those pretty limbs, let us

find a night in the Mediterranean so dark--the stars feel strong enough

to do what they were built for. From the window we can watch

as they talk to the ocean, the black waves using our bodies

to say the words back to them.

Mercury

some days

when he wants to

he has nothing to say

there is no shiver

no silver spine

speaking in scales

he polishes his tongue

waiting for some kind of heaviness to return

the cars move like fast fragments

he sleeps in his old bed

feels nothing

dreams strangely

and in the morning

is woken by the sounds of men

tearing up the concrete with their machines

turning the dirt over

and over

mixing its songs in with the broken stone

failing lessons

how I miss

the shape of your bra

empty

rising over some article of furniture

awakening yesterday

on your mother's couch

through the door

I saw it sitting in your room

you were sleeping

curled into the shape of a

something that

I don't have the imagination anymore for to describe

a serengeti

a strait

a pear slice on a plate

in your sleep

you curl like

you are fighting something off

or waiting to be brought in

a hair

on a doorknob

I have scars hanging off of some girl's ceiling fan

I grabbed the tea kettle too many times

this is how I learned not to touch things

your body always

always makes me want to break that

girl

rewrap me in your white sheets

give me a flashlight

make me glow

grow me peaches

feed them to me

tell me what the sky can mean

show me how to jump into the middle of the lake

show me how to get the stones from the deepest part

and how to then leave them on the shore

make me want to make a child

make me firebomb a building with a bullhorn and a poem

draw me a picture of what smoking a cigarette feels like

kiss me with how much you love the giraffe

give me a hug

a smile shaped like a zoo

show me how to make cotton candy

tell me a story

tell me something you've never told anyone else

help me remember the things I've never told anyone else

the trees outside curve like they have nothing else to say to one another

while behind them the cars keep driving north

why do people talk like they know anything about something

What he wants

is the sun strong on the grass, turning it into gold.

To have a house that holds him in silence.

For the world to forget he was ever inside of it.

A pack of kids he made or gave a life to,

running like hungry dogs through the trees.

He wants a weathervane on the roof, a rooster made of black iron,

to tell him from which direction God is watching.

He wants a woman in whose face he no longer feels ashamed.

A pair of hands that still pray with all they have.

And a rifle hanging over the front door—to take down on New Year's

and shoot empty bottles with,

to use for when the strangers come,

to protect all that he sees from their backward fingers.

He practices in the woods,

placing bullets into bark,

wondering if he could hear their hearts, would he still be able to shoot.

He dirties his hands, plants things in the plentiful dirt.

Breaks the gun into pieces instead, and plants the pieces as well.

A tree of soft cherries

grows from that spot.

When the men come

to take this all,

he and his will sit in the shade of the cherries, eating fruit.

Juice

staining their fingers.

Spitting the pits and laughing loudly instead.

Take us if you must, we were already there.

Till then,

she holds him in her arms while she sleeps.

And he

stares at the moon.

Feeling its hands crawl over him.

Each night trying to feel a little more comfortable in this farm of his.

Tomorrow there will be a meteor shower.

They will go into the blackness to watch it.

Count how many they see streaking across the dark.

Wish on every one of them and say those wishes out loud.

in the haystack I dreamed of being a dentist for you

I heard a boy in a window one night make a wish on your skin

he wished however far he may be

that he will shoot any and all of the mountain lions that ever come for you

will leave a coat built from rabbits on your doorstep for when you are cold

and when you are sick

set a bowl of soup on your sill

tap twice

and sit in the haystacks while you drink it down

stay there whittling a whistle until you are sound asleep

and next to your fucking beauty of a face

set that whistle down softly

for you to kiss should you ever need him to come to you

he is chipping away at a star

trying to work it loose out of the large jaw of the night

to bring it back down to your ears

it sounds like you

it has your softness

one night when the two of you were walking down the street

he heard a boy in a window

make a wish on your skin

mistaking it for something else

no mistakes were made

we searched for arrowheads

it was the end of the world

but I still had things to do

in the backyard of the sun

I picked the wheat when it was high

and full of song

the sun would hurt my eyes

in the kitchen

the cats would stare out the window

the little one would rub against my wrist

the kitchen was cool

I would sit there

trying to see if I could hear my blood

moving through my body

at the far end of the farm there was a tree of spoons

they dangled from the branches like silver windchimes

I kissed Harper under them

we broke a plate and buried the pieces there in the red dirt

her hair was always changing colors

she gave me a tooth she had found

she had actually stolen it out of her brother's room

it had come from one of the cows

we pretended it was from Mars

she put it in my hand

and pressed both her palms tight over mine

whispered

don't go

for now don't go and when you do

take me

when the sun sleeps

take me under its eyelids

take me

as a laugh in its face

I could see the horse sticking its backside out the stable

its tail swinging like a watch

I told her I needed to get back to work

she smiled and went home

I traced the sundial with my thumb

there was a mockingbird sitting on the twelve

I threw a rock at it

missed on purpose

I stood over my father's grave

and cut my palm open wide

the sun went down to touch him

I squeezed out the blood

made a wish on the fallen drops

and thought of a girl

I wish I could bury you

keep you warm

I ate a dinner of bread and ham

then went up to my room

sat in bed with a book

until the book left me

like a stone waiting to flipped

I lay there quietly

the bed held me like a widow

the white sheets made whiter under the moon's hands

I listened for something in the distance

perhaps coming closer

perhaps I would imagine it

a fist of pebbles touched the window

it was Harper

she climbed up the ladder

there was a black blanket on the bed

we pulled it over our arms

kissed each other beneath it

it stretched tight over us

we couldn't see a thing

it was too dark

it felt like the night was closing in on us

we did the only thing that two people with soft hearts

can do on the last day of it all

the bed creaked like the stars outside

they shot themselves at the earth

trying to get here faster

the mice

when the clock slows

to where the afternoon

pulls you down

unrolling you out on the couch

and sleep rolls itself over you like a cloud over the sun

while outside

the sirens wail

like the big men are playing games with themselves

my dreams fall from head

to the floor

pink

soft and eyeless

they sit

eating the carpet because it is in front of their faces

when I wake and get up

they scatter

blindly

bringing their black eyes with them

I hear them hiding in the walls

I been putting peanut butter on crackers

trying to coax them back on out

Acknowledgements

Thank you Derrick for your patience, your support, and most importantly your friendship--you always continue to give inspiration--Sandy and the Parlance crew for the opportunities and understanding you've shared with me, the Portland gang for being there with me over the past ten years, Shokufeh for being my number one fan and to you and Naysan for being there should I need you.

Thank you Mom and Pop for never saying it's time to put art behind you and instead learning me in how important books are, I love you, all this is yours.

And thank you Sarah, for willing to hold the little I had to give and for giving me too much in return to thank you for with these too few words.

Some of these poems previously appeared in the WriteBloody anthology, *The Last American Valentine*.

About the Author

Anis Mojgani is the two time National Poetry Slam Individual Champion of 2006 & 2005, one of only two people to win the title more than once. He also won first place at France's 2007 World Cup Poetry Slam and placed second at the 2007 Individual World Poetry Slam, held in Vancouver B.C. He has been a resident of the Oregon Literary Arts Writer's-In-The-Schools program and has appeared on HBO and NPR. Anis' work has appeared in Rattle Literary Journal and alongside the works of US Poet Laureates Ted Kooser and Billy Collins, in the anthology Spoken Word Revolution Redux. Originally from New Orleans, he currently lives in a white house in Portland, Oregon, with three guys and a cat named Ivan, where he sometimes has a beard and sometimes does not.

OTHER GREAT WRITE BLOODY BOOKS

THE LAST AMERICAN VALENTINE: ILLUSTRATED POEMS TO SEDUCE AND DESTROY
24 authors, 12 illustrators team up for a collection of non-sappy love poetry
Edited by Derrick Brown

SOLOMON SPARROWS ELECTRIC WHALE REVIVAL
Poetry Compilation
*by Buddy Wakefield, Anis Mojgani, Derrick Brown, Dan Leamen
& Mike McGee*

I LOVE YOU IS BACK
Poetry compilation (2004-2006)
by Derrick Brown

BORN IN THE YEAR OF THE BUTTERFLY KNIFE
Poetry anthology, 1994-2004
by Derrick Brown

DON'T SMELL THE FLOSS
New Short Fiction Pieces
by Matty Byloos

THE CONSTANT VELOCITY OF TRAINS
New Poetry
by Lea Deschenes

HEAVY LEAD BIRDSONG
New Poems
by Ryler Dustin

UNCONTROLLED EXPERIMENTS IN FREEDOM
New Poems
by Brian Ellis

LETTING MYSELF GO
Bizarre God Comedy & Wild Prose
by Buzzy Enniss

CITY OF INSOMNIA
New Poetry
by Victor D. Infante

JUNGLESCENE: UNDERGROUND DANCING IN LOS ANGELES
A sweaty modern photographic historical journey
by Danny Johnson

WHAT IT IS, WHAT IT IS
Graphic Art Prose Concept book
by Maust of Cold War Kids and author Paul Maziar

MISS BLISS AND THE LOST RED NIGHT
New Poems
by Mindy Nettifee

NO MORE POEMS ABOUT THE MOON
NON-Moon Poems
by Michael Roberts

CAST YOUR EYES LIKE RIVERSTONES INTO THE EXQUISITE DARK
New Poems
by Danny Sherrard

LIVE FOR A LIVING
New Poetry compilation
by Buddy Wakefield

SOME THEY CAN'T CONTAIN
Classic Poetry compilation
by Buddy Wakefield

SCANDALABRA
(Winter 2008)
New poetry compilation
by Derrick Brown

ANIMAL BALLISTICS
(Winter 2008)
New Poetry compilation
by Sarah Morgan

COCK FIGHTERS, BULL RIDERS, AND OTHER SONS OF BITCHES
(Winter 2008)
An experimental photographic odyssey
by M. Wignall

THE WRONG MAN
(Winter 2009)
Graphic Novel
by Brandon Lyon & Derrick Brown

YOU BELONG EVERYWHERE
(Winter 2009)
A memoir and how to guide for travelling artists
by Derrick Brown with Joel Chmara, Buddy Wakefield, Marc Smith, Andrea Gibson, Sonya Renee, Anis Mojgani, Taylor Mali, Mike McGee & more.

www.writebloody.com

WRITEBLOODY
QUALITY AMERICAN BOOKS AND PRINTING

PULL YOUR BOOKS UP BY THEIR BOOTSTRAPS

Write Bloody Publishing distributes and promotes great books of fiction, poetry and art every year. We are an independent press dedicated to quality literature and book design, with offices in LA, NYC and Murfreesboro, TN.

Our employees are authors and artists so we call ourselves a family. Our design team comes from all over America: modern painters, photographers and rock album designers create book covers we're proud to be judged by.

We publish and promote 8-12 tour-savvy authors per year. We are grass-roots, D.I.Y., bootstrap believers. Pull up a good book and join the family. Support independent authors, artists and presses.

Visit us online:

WRITEBLOODY.COM

CPSIA information can be obtained at www.ICGtesting.com
Printed in the USA
266856BV00001B/3/P